# 10 Things Every Christian Hip Hop Artist Should Know

by Brinson

ISBN 9781535384384

# CONTENTS

# INTRODUCTION:

Hip-hop music has been around for over 30 years. Christian hip hop (CHH) has been around for about 25 years. Currently, there is a lot of attention on Christian rappers and the CHH industry because lots of money is being made by top artists in the genre. Major labels and media outlets are searching for the "Next Big Christian hip hop artist."

Today there are hundreds of thousands of Christian rappers all over the world. You may happen to be one of the people who love God and have chosen the special mission to spread the story of Jesus and His doctrine through your music. This is a great thing because the laborers are few and the harvest is great - just like the Bible says in Luke 10:2.

Besides ministry, there's another side of the coin that many artists need to know about. Hopefully after reading this book you will be able to guard your heart, safeguard, and "faith guard" your music ministry as you do the work of the Lord. My hope is to give you simple concepts, instructions, and warnings, through Biblical principles that will help you not only expand your ministry, but keep your eyes open to its realities.

Music in general has a funny way of putting artists into a fantasy world that doesn't exist. So when real life situations approach, they get offended, leave the church, or (even worse) leave the faith - because what they envisioned music ministry to be is not the reality.

# 1 GUARD YOUR HEART

*Guard your heart above all else, for it determines the course of your life.*
*Proverbs 4:23 (NLT)*

When I started writing this book, chapter one (1) was scheduled to be chapter ten (10). But when I looked at the table of contents, I realized that this section about guarding your heart should be placed at the very beginning because it is so important.

There are many scriptures regarding the heart, and one that sticks out is "a dream deferred makes the heart sick" (Proverbs 13:12 NLT). That is so true; I have been in Christian rap ministry full time for almost 10 years. From that experience I can tell you that there will be days when you feel like the whole world, friends, family, and possibly even the church are against you. I have also witnessed some of the best rappers get offended and leave the faith. Their whole attitude about ministry changed because they did not protect their heart as the Bible teaches.

You have to get clarity about doing Christian rap before you do it. Just like any other ministry, if you are not called to do this, it will rip you apart from the inside out. I have peace about doing this ministry. If you want peace, you need to have a heart-to-heart with God.

Guarding your heart is immersing yourself (spending extensive time) in prayer at every turn. Daily communication with God will do wonders for your career and for you as a believer. His still, small voice will keep you from making bad deals, help you keep a level head, build your patience for dealing with people, and keep your mission in the forefront.

I have seen the good, the bad, and the ugly. One thing is for sure, when you are not consistent in your spiritual routine of prayer, meditating on the Word, and devotional time, your day will not be as great as it could be. Read your Bible. Get closer to the Lord. Study to show yourself approved by rightly dividing the Word of Truth. I am not saying you have to memorize every single Proverb, but you should have some depth in your ministry. This is Christian Hip Hop after all and there should be some evidence of the character and teachings of Christ in your life and music.

I remember a former secular rapper who was newly saved. I saw him at concerts and in the streets grinding and pushing his mixtapes. He believed that he was going to blow up, so he put his trust in his talent rather than putting his trust in The One who was the subject of his rhymes. A year later - he'd stopped going to church, his family had broken apart, and he'd returned to secular rap and the club scene.

What happened to him? He didn't get grounded in the Word. In Mark 4, Jesus talks about the four types of soil and how some people will get saved and excited but don't get deep-rooted in the Word and therefore do not last very long. When you hear the Word, pray that your heart would be good ground and that you receive the harvest from that word.

## Action Steps

Guarding your heart takes a lot of inner building. Here are four things you need to do:

1. Write a vision statement for your ministry. This not only gives clarity to your mission, but it will put you back on track when times get rough. They will certainly get rough. When you ask yourself, "Why am I even doing this?" you can look to the mission that the Lord has given you.

2. Cast down every high thought and imagination that puts itself over the Word of God (2 Corinthians 10:5 NLT). Negative words and thoughts will come, but you have to know how to fight them. Jesus is our perfect example of how to combat anything that is unlike what you are believing God for. When you have negative thoughts speak the Word to neutralize them.

3. Disconnect. Turn off what people and social media are saying. There will always be critics – especially online. Trolls exist. Don't feed them. And talking about your "haters" to others only gives them more power. Turn off the noise and focus on what God says about you. Develop thicker skin. Everyone may not like your music, so what? The answer is to find the people who love your music and believe that God will lead you to them and them to you.

4. Plan to Recharge. While in ministry Jesus himself took time away from his followers to spend time with God. You need to do the same. When I first started GodChaserz, I worked at it for four years straight before I even thought about taking time off. Looking back over all the time and effort I poured into the ministry, I regret not taking a true Sabbath more often. When you recharge, you get fresh ideas. You give God time to speak to you when your mind isn't cluttered.

Prayer:

*"God, I ask you to protect this heart of mine. I believe you gave me this talent to use for Your kingdom. Help me to keep my motives pure and my heart right before You. I need You in all that I do. In Jesus' name, amen!"*

# 2 GROW YOUR BRAND: PROMOTE, PROMOTE, PROMOTE

Over the years I have met a ton of talented Christian artists but after meeting them once, I never saw or heard from them again. This is a huge problem in our genre. So what do we do to fix it?

The Vision dies when YOU stop working. When you stop making new music, stop making contacts, stop utilizing social media, it is because you don't believe anymore. No one can promote YOU better than YOU. You have to make a plan in order to get your music out there. The burden is on your shoulders, but you can do it! I want to stir up the "get up and go" inside of you - the part that has been sleeping, waiting on something to happen. The wait is over. Reading this book is the wakeup call! Do you really believe you are called to do this? If the answer is yes, then let's put that faith into action!

I encourage you to start promoting off line first. Promoting music online is great, but it is also a shot in the dark. Making face to face connections is where it's at. I consider myself an expert at guerilla grassroots promotions, and let me tell you, this type of promoting will never let you down. It's harder than sitting at your computer spamming everyone, but it will have a greater impact because people will see who you are. The next section will cover a few things you can do with your music offline to get your music into the hands of the people. (This list assumes that you already have physical copies of your album, EP, single, or download cards)

## Action Steps

1. Find local events to participate in. When I released my first album, I didn't know where to take my music. I had to listen to Gospel radio stations to find out what was happening in my city. I connected with one of the radio personalities, DJ Souljah, who also hosted a Gospel Skate night each Sunday.

I went to event to see what is was like and discovered that it was a great place to mingle and promote. I found out the details and cost (you have to count the cost on every move you make) for setting up a vending table. The next Sunday, my crew and I set up a merchandise table at the Gospel Skate Night. I did that for almost a year, selling about 50 percent of my inventory at the skate night events. I even got to perform live a few times as well.

Gospel Skate night proved to be a great way to promote my music and get exposure in an unconventional way. I've also had success with local festivals, on college campuses and definitely at church youth nights. I'm sure there are things happening in your city that you don't know about. If you are saying "Not in my city, nothing ever happens here." you can always spend a few bucks and go to a city close to you. Just remember that opportunities to connect locally do exist, you just have to look.


2. It is vitally important that you network to promote your music. You have to attend conferences, festivals and tours outside of your city, and talk to the people who are coordinating or working at these events. Find a connection with them beyond just music. Do you have shared interests or mutual acquaintances? Industry leaders have thousands of artists clamoring for their attention. They are people first and would appreciate a more genuine approach.

Afterwards, cultivate these relationships without spamming. Ask simple questions about their work and how you can help with future events. They may need a host or an emcee or another service you can provide.


3. Hand out sample CDs at your school, a local store, the gym, or your church, with all your contact information.

I remember the first Christian rap CD I purchased. I had just moved to Nashville, TN, where I attended Belmont University. I went to the superstore to pick up a few things. I didn't even make it to the door when a guy rolled up in his car asking if I would buy one of his CDs. He held out what I thought was a secular album but the artwork was killer, so I was interested (You must have great artwork. The professional look always wins!). He asked me for $10 but I only had $5 and he said that he would be crazy not to take it. I got home and popped his CD in my system, and to my surprise it was a gospel rap compilation. The mixing and mastering was great, and I had just found a new artist that I really liked. His name was K-Lee and his hustle was for real!

I also recall two brothers in my city who set up at a local Wal-Mart every day. They had a table and would spend time talking to people, praying with them, and selling CD's. Sometimes you've got to hustle the old fashioned way and let the people know what you are doing and who you are doing it for. They met a lot of people and got their names out there. While this strategy make not work for everyone or in every market, it can be effective.

4. Promote your brand/ministry on everything. It's called branding. Once you have an established name and logo, it needs to be repeated consistently. The more people see your ministry's name, the more they will recognize who you are and what you do. Brand CDs, t-shirts, flyers and stickers (basically, whatever you can put a logo on). It is often said that people have to "see" your brand three times before they remember who you are. That is an important point. Don't assume everyone knows who you are. You have to introduce yourself over and over and over again. Additionally, if you have a unique look or "catch phrase" make sure that is highlighted regularly as well.

If you are just starting out, resist the temptation to keep changing the look of your brand. The exception would be if you realize that your logo, artwork or photos are unprofessional. Enlist the services of a designer to help create the look and feel of your brand. Once you have the right look, be consistent in promoting it.

Promoting as a Christian artist is a struggle. As independent artists, we don't have a big record label spending thousands of dollars on our music. You have to do most of the leg work. Since social media is the most widely used communication tool, let's look at a few things you can do online.

## Additional Action Steps: Promoting Online

5. Build a website. Many people say that social media makes an artist website irrelevant. However, you don't own your social media pages. Social media sites make changes every day, and someone else is regulating what you can and cannot do. A website is your cyber real estate, you can do what you want with it. You can sell your music how you want or give it away, you can even do both. Social Media music sites only let you link to digital music outlets. But what If you have t-shirts (which I highly recommend) to sell, or stickers, buttons and coffee mugs? You can't do all of that on social media. Find a company that creates professional websites or create a simple one yourself (if you have the skills to do so).

6. Find your online audience. You have to identify your target audience. Look for new supporters but don't forget the people who have supported you from the beginning. While there aren't tons, there are several websites, blogs and podcasts that strictly promote Christian Hip Hop. Do your research and look for the ones that cater to your style of music. Once you've identified your target audience find out how you can submit music, an interview request or advertising. Speaking of advertising, I don't recommend spending your entire promo budget on a single website. Artists think that if they are on one particular website, then they've got it made. No sir! We'll dive further into this thought in Chapter 7, One Move Is Not the Answer.

7. Build an email list. One of the most important things I've learned about promoting is having a strong email list. This enables you to communicate directly with your fans. Whenever you have a new song or a new project, the people on this list should hear about it first. Creating amazing content is key if you want people to stay subscribed and forward your emails to their friends, family, and colleagues that aren't already on your list.

Each year your list will lose contacts as people switch email addresses or op-out of communication. As an independent artist, it is your job to constantly add new contacts so you can keep your numbers moving up. There is extensive information available online about how to keep your email list fresh.

8. Utilize social media. This is one of the simplest things to do but it takes strategy to do it well. First, you MUST be consistent. There is so much content online that the only way to stand out over time is being visible and consistent.

There are tools available to help you set up automatic messages for certain times of the day or to send one message to Facebook, Twitter, Instagram or Google Plus etc. at the same time.

You aren't just selling music, you are inviting people into your world. I asked myself "what do you love to do?" That's easy; I love to minister, to travel, and to eat. That is what you will find on my social media posts. I post about loving Jesus, traveling for ministry and eating in new places that I've never been before. Your top 3 may be different; but whatever you love, the people who follow you and love your music may find a connection with that too.

These steps will grow your brand. Do not despise your small beginning, as the Bible teaches. Don't hate where you are! Everyone had to start somewhere. Jesus had to start small; he didn't start off with 12 men following him. He had to be faithful at his local church, grow in understanding, get his miracle flow up, and THEN he went into the ministry. Jesus was 30 years old before he went on tour, so don't be too hard on yourself. Realize that it will take faith, grit and hard work! You will have to encourage yourself along the way. But remember, God will help you and open doors for you!

Prayer:

*Father God, Thank you for giving me these gifts and talents to use for Your Glory; You said in Your Word that I can do all things through Christ Jesus who strengthens me. Now Lord, I ask for that strength to promote, strength to grind, strength to reach heights, and strength to encourage others. God, I know I have to put action behind my faith, help me not to be slack or lazy. I know you are with me and I pray for success in all that I do in your name. You gave Your Son for this world, help me to spread the Gospel message with power, clarity, and love. In Jesus name I pray, Amen.*

*For when we persevere with Him, He makes everything beautiful in its time (Ecclesiastes 3:11).*

# 3 PROMOTE JESUS

*For whosoever shall be ashamed of me and of my words, of him shall the Son of man be ashamed, when he shall come in his own glory, and in his Father's, and of the holy angels. Luke 9:26*

My pastor, Michael T. Smith, preached a message entitled "God Firstness". It really encouraged me to bless the name of Jesus as soon as I wake up, throughout the day, and in all that I do. Let me encourage you to promote Jesus in everything you do with your music. Promote him on your album cover, at your concerts, on your tees, and all of your merchandise.

Sometimes being a gospel artist means you have to be a cut above the rest. I remember being at a mainstream event where I was the only gospel rapper. It was very evident who I was representing. Everything from what I said to what I sold represented Jesus. Several people came by my table and complimented my CD's artwork and asked questions about my ministry. Right then - it hit me. There are more people for me than against me.

So many Christians falsely believe they won't be well received when they go out. That's simply not true! In dark places, people are always drawn to the light. When you raise the Jesus banner, people gather around to see it for themselves. People are looking for a "sign" to lead them to or back to God. You could be the sign! Let your music say "Hey, God loves you and you are on His mind!"

When I travel, I ask for God's protection and for an opportunity to share Jesus first and then my music with someone. Only God knows how many albums I've sold on Amazon, iTunes, or Google Play because I talked about Jesus in an airport, on a plane, or in the mall.

The Bible talks about the power in the name of Jesus. Things happen when we use that precious name. That means your music can be a forerunner for the miraculous. When spiritual things intersect with the natural realm miracles appear.

Don't be ashamed of the one who saved you. Sing about Him, rap about Him, and let Him draw people to you so you can point them back to Him. When "God Firstness" is the heart of your music - your best comes forth. My prayer is that your best comes forth after reading this book.

## Action Steps

**Here are some ways to promote Him in your music ministry:**

1.  Be a Christian. The Word says "IF you love me you will keep my commandments." It doesn't say "be perfect" but we should always strive to be like Him. Your lifestyle will promote Jesus in a way that your music can't. People will look for flaws. Live your life above reproach as much as you can. Be a Jesus follower to the core. Live by the Word.

2. If you teach or preach, sample a message of yourself speaking and put it into your songs.

3. Tell people you are a Christian or gospel rapper. Be vocal about what you do! People want to see someone who stands for something (even if they share our faith).

4. Remix an old hymn and put your spin on it. Remixes are a great way to connect with people who love a popular song but don't know you.

5. Create an anthem promoting Jesus then make a sticker and a tee shirt that corresponds with it. One powerful thing about being a Christian rapper is that you can make every single song about Jesus and it's alright. Think about DC Talk's "Jesus Freak" (1995) - that was a generation-changing song, maybe one of the biggest Christian songs of this century. It is still in regular rotation today! Making a hit single about Jesus is a great move.

6. Make a spoken word (acapella rap) video/interlude. We know that viral videos can take an unknown person and put them in millions of households overnight. You can make a simple video on camera talking about Jesus and who He is to you. Then you can take the audio and place it on your album. Some listeners are more inclined to listen to words first before they give your music a chance. Spoken word is a powerful tool.

These ideas should give your creativity a boost when thinking about promoting Jesus. Take a few moments to meditate on how much you love God and how you can share Him with the world.

Prayer:
*Father, Thank you for loving me. Thank you for giving me this desire to tell the world about you and your everlasting goodness. I praise You with joyful lips and a joyful heart. God, I Thank you that I bear much fruit in all that I do. I now pray over the ears, eyes, and minds of those I will speak to concerning you, oh God. I pray that their hearts are good ground to sow the seed of faith. I know that man plants and waters but God You alone give the increase. I pray for an increase and harvest of lives transformed by You. Lord, your goodness and mercy endures forever and Thank you right now for it all. I love you and I Thank you for loving us first. In Jesus' name. Amen.*

# 4 GOD WILL HELP YOU

This is something you need to know: God is truly on your side. I know, you're saying "Of course He is Brinson, I work for Him." I'm making this statement not only because you need to be reminded, but because the reality is, other Christian rappers may not help you become successful.

I know you want to believe that we are all on the same team and that we'll all help each other. In truth, many artists on the top Christian Hip Hop labels may not even notice you. This is the only genre where most artists do not help each other. Chapter one talks about guarding your heart, and this is one of the reasons why.

Think about the average Christian rapper who sells less than 100 albums per release. For example, imagine a new rapper named D'Maskus who just finished up his album. Next, we have a guy named Fresh Praise Dude (FPD), who is signed to a big Christian rap label. D'Maskus runs into FPD on his big label tour and he asks him, "How can I grow my ministry?" In response, FPD, who knows his label spent $50,000 on marketing and promoting his last album simply answers "Just stay faithful and God will bless it."

Was that a true statement? Yes, it was. Was it the whole truth? No, it wasn't. He could have given him details of what his label does but he chose otherwise. There are thousands of Christian rappers and only about 20 are on labels with big enough budgets to truly stay visible. The point is, don't expect other rappers to help you, (some will) but you must rely on God's leading and direction.

God will help you along the way. God knew you would answer the call to uplift His people and He has people in place, assigned to specific stages of your career to carry you through hard times and to take you to the next level.

Ministry has ups and downs, but you have to take the good with the bad and be thankful for both. While pursuing this call, you'll have a family, bills, and other life situations. You have to make sure you stay afloat as you flow for God. In my experience, there were many times when money got tight - even super tight. There were periods when I didn't have any shows coming up, and my iTunes and digital sales were not looking great. I had bills past due and then the phone would ring with a message saying I got booked for a concert. The person on the line said that the Lord led them to book me. Now nobody knew what my situation was, but God did. He has done things like that more times than I can count.

Doubt is a strong enemy, but the comfort of God's help is greater. When things like bills and the other pressures of life pile up on you and you know in your heart of hearts that you are giving your all to God - your faith hits the doorstep of Heaven and our God always has a way of showing that He is there and is more than able to take care of His own. Amen.

There are people that have what you need and God will touch them to release those things to you. When I was making my first ever music video for "Solar Powered" I didn't have a huge budget. The label wasn't selling a ton of music, but I was making good money from concerts. I had allotted a whopping $800, which was a lot for me at the time. It may as well been $50,000, that's how much it was to me back then.

I met a local filmmaker who charged me $500 for the video. Then I rented a new Christian studio to shoot it in. My oldest brother helped me out and purchased the ticket for my homie D-M.A.U.B. to come down from Cincinnati just for the shoot.

It was a crazy night. We had all these people standing around waiting to get into the studio. One hour went by, then two. I remember that I had to have my "poker face" on and not look worried because everyone was looking at me. I stepped away from the crowd of people who had come out for the video so I could pray. I prayed to God like "Lord, I need you RIGHT NOW! Help your boy out!"

The owner of the studio finally showed up two hours after the start time we agreed upon. He wasn't in the best frame of mind, but he came through and we shot the video. After we wrapped shooting he told me to keep my money – no charge. I didn't ask questions. I shook his hand and told him Thank you. The video shoot was important to me even though it was a financial sacrifice. But

God is always on time and He does things His way. We just gotta know that He is truly in control.

Prayer:

*God, Thank you for being GOD! A big God and an awesome God! Thank you that you will never leave me nor forsake me. You are a high tower and fortress! Thank you for giving up your only son to die for my sins and Thank you for your grace that never fails in my life. I receive all of your blessings, protection, promises, and goodness today and forever. Thank you Jesus for always being an ever-present help in my personal life and ministry. In Jesus' name, Amen.*

# 5 IT'S ABOUT THE PEOPLE

*For I know the thoughts that I think toward you, saith the LORD, thoughts of peace, and not of evil, to give you an expected end. Jeremiah 29:11 (KJV)*

The target of the Gospel message you preach should always be the heart of the listeners God blesses you to speak into. You may be the greatest rapper in the world, but it is not about you. Yes, God has blessed you with a gift - but it has a purpose. You may be able to rap, sing, play instruments, produce fire beats, and perform like the late, great, Michael Jackson; but it's all to draw people to Jesus.

You may say "I know this, Brinson" but there are plenty of artists trying to photo bomb Jesus while He is getting His glory. A lot of us are intellectuals. We know the scriptures very well and that draws people to us. Never take the credit. Always direct accolades and praise back to Him. Remember that it is the Lord who gave you whatever gifts you have in the first place. Please don't allow any of those things to cloud your judgment when it comes to ministry. God has blessed you to bless His people.

*For God is working in you, giving you the desire and the power to do what pleases Him. Phil. 2:13 NLT*

One of my good friends, Nate "Champ" Harvey told me once, "We all are one decision away from losing it all." Meaning, you can make one bad move and lose your ministry, tarnish your name, and be out of the game.

*"So, if you think you are standing firm, be careful that you don't fall!" 1 Cor. 10:12 (NIV)*

People are so important for you as an artist. I have always tried to love people to the best of my ability. When people talk to me after a concert I give them my full attention (whether they buy merch or not). We, as artists, don't know what someone has gone through just to come to our concert. I remember a lady and her two kids came to a listening party I held. One of the artists who invited her didn't mention that there was an entry fee. She said she didn't have any money to get all three of them in. Plus see had driven a long way to get there. Do you think she didn't get in to the concert? Of course she did! And her kids got a ton of free stuff.

This should be common practice, however, the reality is that your favorite artist may not be the person you think they are. Music creates connection, it makes us feel like we really know the person on the mic. But that is not the case. Some artists feel like they can just do whatever, whenever, and to whomever. It is heartbreaking that some artists are not representing Jesus Christ by loving on God's people.

I have so many stories of people at concerts saying "Brinson, you are not like the other rappers. You actually care about the people." One rule I always share with up-and-coming artists is: Always show love to the people (because they are God's people *and* they didn't have to book you or come to your concert). We all should be a beacon of light for anyone who comes in contact with us.

As artists/ministers of the Gospel, we must take care of the people. If you feel moved to pray with them, then PRAY! Make them laugh, make them smile, be a part time counselor. Always ask God to give you the words to say. Your gifts work the best when there are hurting people in the crowd. Believe that you are God's conduit to channel goodness to His people.

I met a young guy named Dylan while in California taping several shows for TBN (Trinity Broadcasting Network). We talked and laughed and I told him a funny story about my snapback cap addiction. I showed him nearly 20 hats I'd carried in my bag. His eyes lit up and I knew I had to pass on a few hats to the little guy. I gave him 2 snapbacks and taught him how to wear them.

After showing love to him, I later received an email from his mom thanking me. She said little Dylan needed a smile because he was having a hard time making friends at school. He needed someone to show him the love of Christ. Guess what? God loved on him. He will never forget that a bearded rap guy came into his life, gave him all the attention in the world, told him he mattered and that God loves him.

I got a supporter for life and he loves my music. But more importantly, he got a steroid shot of faith early in his life. Just imagine what a 9-year-old kid on fire for God can do! He has many good years ahead of him to impact this world. Even right now, I'm praying that Dylan's life is blessed beyond measure and that God will use him greatly!  It's about the people!

*Let your light so shine before men, that they may see your good works, and glorify your Father which is in heaven. Matt. 5:16*

You should base how you love people on how Jesus did it during his time of ministry. He went out among the people. He healed them, prayed for them, gave encouragement, and even forgave people of their sins. I'm not saying that you will lay hands on the sick and they'll recover. (But I'm not excluding that either if that is a part of God's plan for you.)

I do, however, want to give a disclaimer: If you haven't received training from ministry school or your pastor, I would not recommend laying hands on people. If you are new at ministry or just feel uncomfortable, it's okay. When you feel the need to pray, make it a congregational prayer. Or you can write yourself a note, and pray for people on your own at a future time following your encounter. Finally, I recommend that you pray before every concert. Having heaven's endorsement is the only way to help the people because it is about them.

Remember, this is Christian Hip Hop - meaning it is rooted in the Gospel of Jesus Christ. I have seen a lot of artists careers cut short because they were not rooted in the things of God. This is why I've included the spiritual aspects of Christian hip hop in addition to lessons learned in the music business.

Prayer:

*Father in the name of Jesus, I Thank you that the Word of God is powerful and active in my life. Thank you that you have given the Spirit of power, love and a sound mind. Lord, help me walk in love, which is walking in you because God is love.*

*Father, I ask that you give me the words to say to your people at every encounter. I ask you to use me to be a light and represent you in a manner that pleases you. I know that this gift you have given me is for the lost sheep and the body of Christ.*

*Thank you for the grace to walk in these gifts. Give me a heart for your people. Help me not to hurt with my words and my actions, but to heal, encourage, uplift, and set people free.*

*Father, you have taken me out of darkness into your light and I ask that as I talk, rap, sing, reach, and preach about you, that you draw men out of darkness! Lord, I Thank you for the understanding of your written word. Thank you for a better relationship with you. Let my great personal time with you spill over to all areas of my ministry. This I ask in Jesus' name. Amen.*

Sit silently for a moment and just listen. The Lord may have something to say to you.

# 6 IT'S STILL A BUSINESS

*"Every business needs to get their business in order"*

*-Dre Murray, Billboard charting artist; Collision Records*

In this chapter we'll discuss money and business. Christian Hip Hop is a ministry but for many artists, it is also their primary income source. This is a topic that needs to be considerable discussion. Is anything wrong with money? No! The love of money is where the problem comes in. All ministries use it to spread the message of Jesus on multiple platforms. It's used to feed the hungry, clothe the homeless, sponsor missionaries, and to purchase plane tickets for Christian rap artists.

Money is a major struggle for Christian artists. They struggle with the challenge of doing ministry and making sure that their purpose isn't primarily for financial gain. The Bible teaches that a worker is worth his wages. But the Bible also cautions us not to be moved by money or love money over the call of God on our lives. You should always do a heart check when deciding on a ministry opportunity. Are you being motivated by the size of the check or are you being led by the Spirit? You have to find a balance between ministering the good news, while making sure that you are taken care of financially.

I consider myself an entertainer with a ministry call. My personal standard is that I will never charge to bring the Gospel message (this is my standard, you have to follow how God leads you). I simply view the two elements of my work differently. To me, preaching or teaching is ministry. Music or being a personality is entertainment. I still allow people to pay for my travel, but to ask for a price to preach the Bible is not a something I charge for. I hope you share the same heart.

When you're dealing with ministries and the word "honorarium" comes up, the mood often changes. Some artists panic and have anxiety about these conversations. My advice is to have someone in your circle who can play a management role. Their role is to go over specifics so you can keep your heart in check while they represent you. If you are okay with having these conversations, it's all good!

I have been cheated out of money in ministry. And I've seen other artists experience the same thing. There are unfortunate stories of labels not paying artists and churches not paying rappers who have committed to travel hundreds of miles to perform in front of their congregation. Why am I discussing negative things in this chapter? Because you must be prepared for everything in ministry.

I know one artist who traveled across the country to rap at a ministry. The pastor who booked him bragged about all the money he spent booking all the major artists to come to his church. But when my friend showed up and performed, he left without a check. Why did this happen? It was because the artist didn't have his ducks in a row. He didn't pre-arrange and plan his trip with any sort of formal agreements or contracts. He didn't request or conduct any actual business meetings with the person who "hired" him.

I want you to get your business in order. Leave nothing to chance or assumptions. You will need contracts and business forms. If you are going to record a feature for an artist and you need to cover expenses (i.e. studio time, travel, etc.) say that UPFRONT. Be clear with every need and request.

I encourage artists to sit down and list what sort of prerequisites they need before accepting a gig. Consider things like your traveling rate. What would you charge to do a guest spot? (Also define what that means to you.) What would you like to receive for hosting an event? These details are usually covered in a standard artist rider (if you don't know what a rider is, you can find a sample online).

## Action Steps

1. Educate yourself. Educate yourself, not just about music, but about business. Whether you like it or not, the government sees your label/ministry

as a business and you need to treat it as such. The difference is that yours is in the mighty hands of the Lord.

You can get basic business education that will be useful in your ministry. If you are in college, or have a college near you, take a business course. Get some sort of business education under your belt. Learning about accounting, management, and basic business software will help your ministry out greatly.

2. Do what you can, hire out the rest.  Some artists find it hard to keep up with the administrative aspects of music business. You may not be best person to write contracts or represent yourself during negotiations, so find someone who can help you. If they have to be paid - pay them. Always be willing to pay people for their time. And remember that hiring someone doesn't take away from your responsibilities. You should always know what's going on with your business even if you hire someone for specific aspects.

3. Diversify your income streams. This is not only about music, but being a good steward over what God has entrusted to you. One of the biggest Christian rap labels in the past ten years is Reach Records. Besides music, they have many other products like clothing, books, DVD teaching series, conferences, and the list goes on and on. They could not have done this without someone behind the scenes who has a mind for business. Utilize their example. See what they do well and how it might apply to your own work. Good old business training will help you with that.

4. Get everything in writing. There are many horror stories from the Christian hip hop community about being taken advantage of on a business level - mainly because they didn't have their business in order. You might say "I don't know where to start." Find someone who is experienced in negotiations to help you. If you have the means, hire a lawyer on a retainer to draw up a few contracts for you. Alternatively, you can always go online and search for music business contract templates that you can use. You can also utilize software to send and

request a digital signature for contracts. This can save you both time and money.

Prayer:

*Father, Thank you for this ministry! I come to you with a grateful heart and thanksgiving today. Lord, your thoughts are higher than my thoughts, and your ways are higher (correct and absolutely right) than my ways.*

*I acknowledge that you know my end from the beginning. I know as far as this ministry and the music industry is concerned, You know where it is going, and it's all in your hands. I place my works before you. I need Your understanding. Help me to be diligent in business. Help me to handle all things related to this ministry in excellence. Help me in my inventory, contracts, accounts, deals, events, bookings, negotiations, and all things under the umbrella.*

*I pray for insight and favor with You, dear God. Thank you for promotion and good success. I receive them both in Jesus' name. Amen.*

# 7 ONE MOVE IS NOT THE ANSWER

When Christian hip hop artists are building their brand, they often think "*If I just had _____ everything would be different.*"
We all have been there. It could be "If I get my songs mixed and mastered by the same company that does _____'s music I will have their sound." Or "If I buy this microphone for my studio I'm going to another level."

When I was building my label and focusing on producing, I would often say "*If this artist copped a beat from me, everyone will hear how dope I am at producing, and the flood gates will open.*" Another time, when I was on touring heavily, I would say "*As soon as I perform on an international stage, everything will change and I will go to the next level.*"

Let me put your mind and heart at ease, one thing will NOT take you to another level. It's the consistency of many things working together that will. No matter who your favorite artist is, you can be sure that they are doing several things simultaneously. They are touring, on the radio, utilizing social media, in fashion/clothing, contests, etc.

A good friend of mine, Big Earl, explained it to me like this. Building an artist is like making a meal - you need different ingredients at different stages. You can't start out with the pepper if it goes in at the end of the recipe. You need the right parts to come together at the right time in order to complete the meal.

The "If I had this" mentality can be an expensive pipe dream. While recording my first solo album, *Escaping Me*, I told myself that I needed to have some well-known guest appearances. I thought that if people saw popular artist on my project they would know I was for real. I reached out to a bunch of artists for features and we made some great music. One particular artist, who was pretty well known at the time, advised me that he usually charged $1,500 for a feature but for me he offered half off. I paid him and after the album was released, I realized that his appearance didn't make much of a difference. It took a long time to break even for that single in digital sales. Having a popular guest feature does not guarantee that your album will be a top seller.

I walked away with a couple of lessons. First, the majority of people who bought my music wanted to hear more of me. Second, is that "famous" is relative. The person in the genre who you think is famous and will draw others to your music, may be virtually unknown to others.

## Action Steps

1. Come to grips with reality. No singular website will make you blow up. One feature from a major artist will not make you blow up. Being on tour will not make you blow up. Getting interviewed on TV or a radio show will not make you. It takes all of these things working together.

2. Create S.M.A.R.T (Specific, Measurable, Achievable, Relevant, Time bound) goals and stick to them.

3. Schedule your goals, three, six, and twelve months in advance. Outline things you can do every three months that will promote you as an artist. The Bible instructs us to write the vision down. For example, if you want to get a specific interview when your single drops, make a list of outlets you want to talk to weeks in advance and start contacting them to schedule times.

4. Develop a whirlwind media blitz. Schedule video and single releases as well as interviews, album reviews and ads to release around the same time. Make a splash.

5. Stay on fire and don't burn out. Promoting is a marathon, not a sprint. After you release your project, plan other promotional activities to keep the buzz going.

6. Evolve into more than just an artist. What else can you do? Can you shoot your own videos? Can you produce your own beats? Can you write a book? Let people know what else God has enabled you to do. Give the Lord more space to work through you.

Prayer:

*Lord Jesus, I Thank you for being the ONE thing that I truly need. You said in Your word that I can do all things through You, Christ alone who strengthens me. I have many tasks to complete on this journey and I need You every step of the way.*

*God, I know that all good things come from You. Thank you for every good thing that You will bring forth in my ministry. Thank you that there is a season for everything under the sun, and right now, I Thank you in advance for the season of prosperity in ministry through Your hand and Your goodness.*

*Thank you for promotion from heaven. Jesus, I love You. Please keep my heart on You as I walk this out. Amen.*

# 8 YOU CAN CHANGE THE GAME

Christian hip hop isn't just about the beats and the rhymes. No, that is the easy part. It's about being an agent of change through your ministry. Many times artists put all of their faith in the success of their music. Then, when the music doesn't produce the fruit they desire, they throw in the towel. But there is so much more you can do to change the game than music.

After reading the proceeding chapters, I imagine that some readers will say "There is nothing in my city or even around me that has anything to do with Christian hip hop. It is so needed here." Since you see the need, you should be the one to bring about change in your city. It may be the Lord tugging at your heart to make an impact in your metropolis. And you, being an Ambassador of Heaven, have a responsibility to impact the lives of people.

Here is a short list of ways you can reshape the game in your city:

## 1. With your music
You understand the people and culture where you live. Make music that will connect with the saints closest to you. If you do any type of outreach ministry, take your music and use it to impact hurting hearts. You don't know what God can do with one of your songs while you're doing what you do.

I have a song called "He Said He Loves Me" and it speaks about how the Lord healed my mother. It is a real faith booster and people need their faith increased. That song is several years old, but to this I still day get testimonies of how that song has touched someone. When your music is connected to the Most High God it will have an everlasting effect on the listeners. God is love and His power to transform is unmatched. When you talk about Him good things should happen.

## 2. Write for a local newspaper, blog, or magazine

Most rappers are also good writers because they can express very strong opinions. You can share the message of the cross in places and to people that your music may not get to. Besides, we need more Christians working in media outlets — particularly the secular ones. As followers of Christ, we cannot withdraw from these areas because our views are counter to mainstream culture. If we do, we'll eventually become mute in that arena.

## 3. Create your own events

I had my first concert when I was 18. I didn't know what I was doing. I got some flyers designed and had radio commercials made to promote the concert. Only about 30 people showed up outside of the other artist on the show, but it was still a win. I continued having concerts and the crowds grew. I learned a lot about concert promoting and how to market events. Then I used those experiences to help with marketing and promoting my music.

Keep in mind you can do concerts almost anywhere. They don't have to be inside of a church. I've seen Christian hip hop concerts in places like city parks, Chick-Fil-A restaurants, rented-out clubs, pool halls, etc. If you want to use a church, it helps to have a good relationship with the pastor so they trust you enough to use their facility. You have to put in the work to promote your concert and not depend on the church or pastor to bring the people. You get out there and make things happen.

## 4. Guest host events

This has to be one of the most overlooked ways to grow your platform. The more people see you - the better. It doesn't matter if you are not rapping. Anytime you have a mic you can tell people that you have a project coming out or where they can find your music. You should always have at least a single out that you can point people to. Just think about it. You are hosting, your name and image is on the flyer - people get to see you in a different capacity.

## 5. Create a radio show

Maybe there is a local radio station in your area that doesn't know about Christian hip hop. You can go to a studio or use your computer to make a 30-minute demo to present to the radio station. Hosting allows you to share your point of view and play the music you love. You also get the bonus of being an on air personality and seen as an expert on Christian hip hop.

## 6. Volunteer

Don't overlook volunteering for a ministry or an organized group that is doing great things in the community. This is ministry at its finest. Volunteering provides an opportunity to reach and touch the people who need you the most.

I have volunteered for homeless shelters, prisons, public schools, private schools, elderly homes, and the list goes on and on. God can place you in key positions where you are the "go-to" artist for major events hosted by an organization. There is a great ministry called CityTakers in Atlanta. They are deeply invested in prison ministry and working with the homeless in their city. They have events where they distribute food and clothes, and offer free concerts. They have become change agents in their city. Many churches call upon them for concerts, speaking engagements, and other events. You may not have heard of them but the hurting people in Georgia know them very well.

Change comes when you have the courage to make things happen. There are many more ways that you can reshape the landscape in your region. You need to use your creativity to raise the bar in your town.

## Prayer:

*Lord, Thank you for changing me! Thank you for people doing ministry all over the world. God, I come to you to ask you to help me be the change in my region. Give me ideas from Heaven! Help me change the game where I am and places across the world through the medium of music and beyond. I know I'm only one person, but with you on my side I have more than enough to carry out this task. God I trust you and lean on you. You said that I shouldn't lean upon my own understanding so I fully rely on you. Be a lamp unto my feet and my path way as you use me for change. In Jesus' name. Amen.*

# 9 YOU GOTTA WORK

Artists have a lot of misconceptions when they enter the Christian Hip Hop music industry. One is that this will be a walk in the park. Let's rewire your thinking for a second. This is a ministry, and ministry requires a lot of work, that means late nights and early mornings. Not just the fun work of going to the studio to make a hot song. No! There's also the work it takes for you to put your music and message into the hands of perfect strangers. And don't forget the work to keep your family's finances afloat as you go forth in this calling.

The good news is: You, my friend, are built for this. The Bible teaches that God won't give you more than you can bear (1 Corinthians 10:13 NIV). Proverbs repeatedly outlines the benefits of diligence versus being lazy. And King Solomon reminds us to consider the work ethic of the ant. You can do this!

A couple of artists whose work ethic I really respect are K-Drama and D-M.A.U.B. Both of these brothers are great rappers, (some of my favorites) and both work super hard. Their grind is amazing. Oh yeah, both of these brothers are also devoted husbands and fathers as well.

Outside of rap, K-Drama is a full-time producer and a pretty good one at that. His work has been featured on many albums – including a few that have been nominated for Stellar and Dove Awards. That is a big deal. He is always touring and doing a great job at staying relevant. He regularly posts about his new beats or has a beat sale.

The same thing goes for D-M.A.U.B. His rap skills are through the roof and he still works hard in other areas. He's the CEO of One Route Entertainment and One Route Films. He also mixes and masters projects for other artists and recently opened a successful clothing line called G(O)OD Company Apparel. Finally, D-M.A.U.B. is now a pastor of a church plant called Love and Grace Outreach.

Being in the Christian music industry is about faith, talent, and relationships. You have to work hard at having all three in top shape. I've learned that if you aren't signed to an active label that is investing $30,000 or more into your project or maintaining a frequent tour schedule, you will need multiple income streams to keep the bills paid while you rap.

Another tip is to make a schedule for each week. Nothing will knock the wind out of an artist faster than feeling unproductive. You look back and a week, a month, or six months have gone by and that single isn't finished or the album is STILL sitting in your computer unmixed.

If you are just starting an album, schedule an hour a day to work on it. Take 30 minutes to write when you wake up and 30 minutes before bed or carve out time on your lunch break. After you've found consistency with setting aside time to write, take a week to research recording studios. Get the pricing and hourly rates (optional: investing in a home studio could save you lots of time and money).

After that week, schedule a day to create a budget including expenses for production, mixing, mastering and promotion (online and offline). This will allow you to calculate the total cost of the project and how long it will take you to secure the necessary funds.  If you are married, you may need to discuss this with your spouse so that you can plan for how to work this budget in with your family's finances.

An artists' work doesn't stop with making and promoting music. The real work begins after a project is released. You have to come up with ways to keep the music fresh. You could release a new single or maybe remix the album. Or release a new music video with a feature with other artists.

The work never stops, so you have to be diligent. You can't stop if you are serious about the music ministry. For example, artists like Kirk Franklin, TobyMac and the Newsboys have all been at the top of the music game since I was in middle school. If the best-selling artists are pushing out albums every year - use their formula. Study how successful artist are scheduling their albums/promotion and follow it on your scale. As the saying goes, "you don't have to reinvent the wheel".

**Prayer:**

*Lord, I Thank you for these hands and that you have made them diligent. God you said, "If a man doesn't work, he doesn't eat." I want to set all of my works before you. I go forth to lift up the name of Jesus. I know there is power in preaching the cross. I receive that power now and walk in the fullness as a child of the Most High God.*

*Jesus, you told the disciples to go into all the corners of the earth making disciples. I take my gifts, works, faith, and being unashamed of the Gospel of Jesus Christ to all parts of the earth that you send me. Everywhere my feet treads I will represent the Kingdom of God all of my days.*

*Lord, I need you to carry out every task along the way. I can do all these things through you. I love you God and I give you my all. In Jesus' name, Amen.*

# 10  IS IT REALLY ABOUT JESUS?

Many Christian rappers didn't start out that way; a lot of them were rapping in secular arenas. Then one day, in the middle of climbing that mountain, God touches their heart to cross over and represent Him with their talents. It's easy to slip back into what motivated you before. Rapping for the world is easy because you're only trying to get money and fame. But when you are a Christian artist, you have to think higher than just financial gain. You have to think about enriching people, expanding the Kingdom and you come last.

We need to analyze why we are doing what we do. Are we doing it for the Kingdom or being self-centered? People will tell you how good you sound, how good you perform, how anointed you are. The praise of men feels good. We must re-direct that praise back to Jesus. I'll say it again. We must re-direct that praise back to Jesus. The more we say "Thank you", the more *we* receive the glory. The more we redirect, the more we acknowledge that this is all a part of God's plan.

Would you give up music if the Lord asked you to? Music is a big part of a lot of artists' lives. We have practiced, gone through trials, invested money, invested emotions, and even sacrificed relationships. We all are believing for something big to happen with our music ministry. But there may come a day when the Lord asks you to put it down for His sake. He may have something else for you - something that doesn't require you to do music anymore. Would you give God a "Yes" or be in rebellion and hold on to the talent you love so much? Would you be able to lay your gift at the altar?

Abraham waited on a son for years and years. The Lord finally blessed him with Isaac in his old age. Then one day the Lord asked him to sacrifice his son as an offering. As the scripture explains, the Lord stopped him. But it was a test of faith and obedience.

Your gift to rap, to sing, to move the crowd - the thing that has been part of your identity your entire life - are you willing to walk away? Are you willing to walk away from the stage, the lights, the studio, the writing sessions, the feeling when you hear that new beat? Would you say "the Lord giveth and the Lord taketh away?" Are you one who says "I am a vessel of God, and where He sends me I go"?

I heard someone say "if God calls you to be a missionary don't settle for being a king." Is it really about Jesus? Because Jesus has the option to set you on another course. He knows where He can use you to your maximum potential.

I'm not suggesting that you stop doing music. I only want to tug at your heart and focus your inner lens back on Jesus. You are a Christian artist, and that means you are Christ-like. Christ was led by the Spirit, the voice of the Father in Heaven. Listen to Heaven's call and where it says go, you say "yes." Don't be a prisoner to the gift and miss the gift giver. Bless God's people, but know God is the one who blesses you, and has blessed you with this gift. He is greater than the gift, and we ought to love him more than anything. As my pastor has taught me - NOTHING ELSE MATTERS BUT GOD!

Made in the USA
San Bernardino, CA
27 December 2016